LEGO NINJAGO®
Masters of Spinjitzu

BUILD YOUR OWN ADVENTURE

CONTENTS

LLOYD'S MECH

Meet Lloyd, the Green Ninja. He is part of a Ninja team that protects the Ninjago world from evil. Any bad guys had better beware, because Lloyd has got a new and powerful Ninja Mech. Its long arms are equipped with shining swords, and its legs are plated with tough, green armor. Will any of the Ninja's enemies dare take it on?

INSTRUCTIONS FOR LLOYD'S MECH

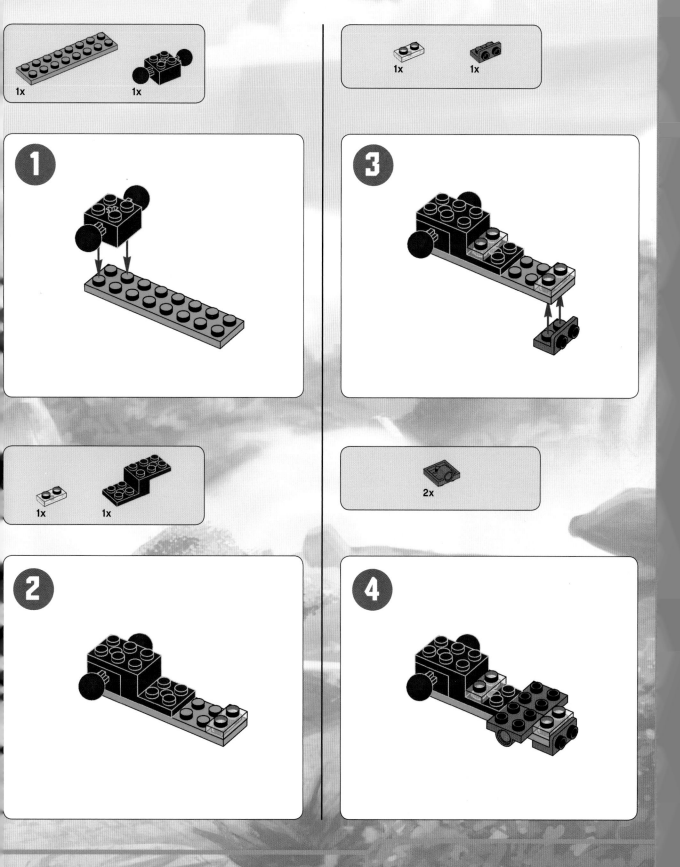

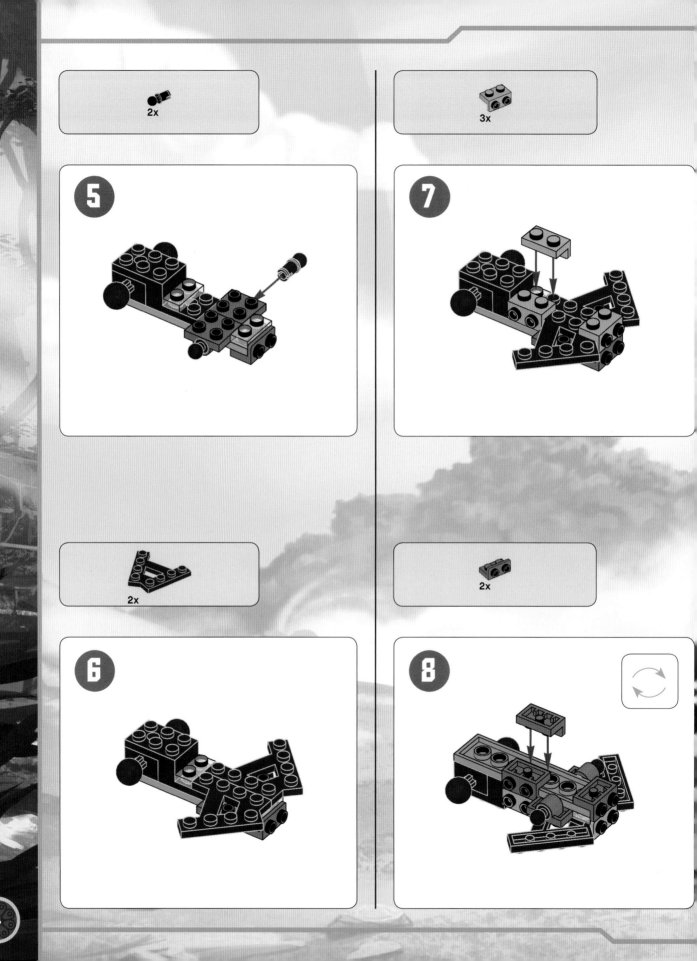

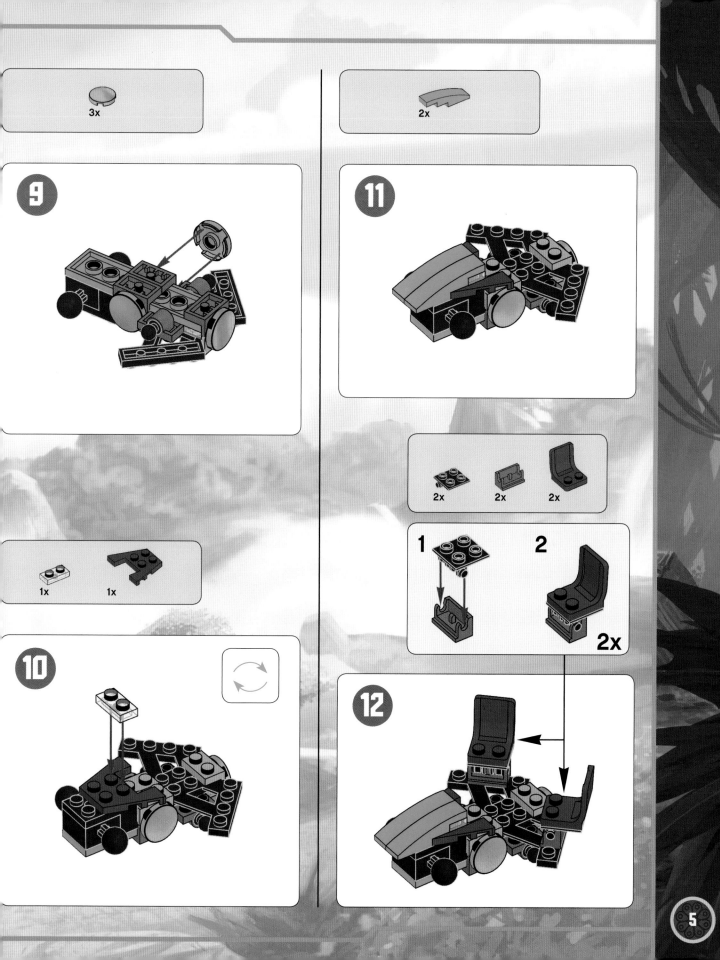

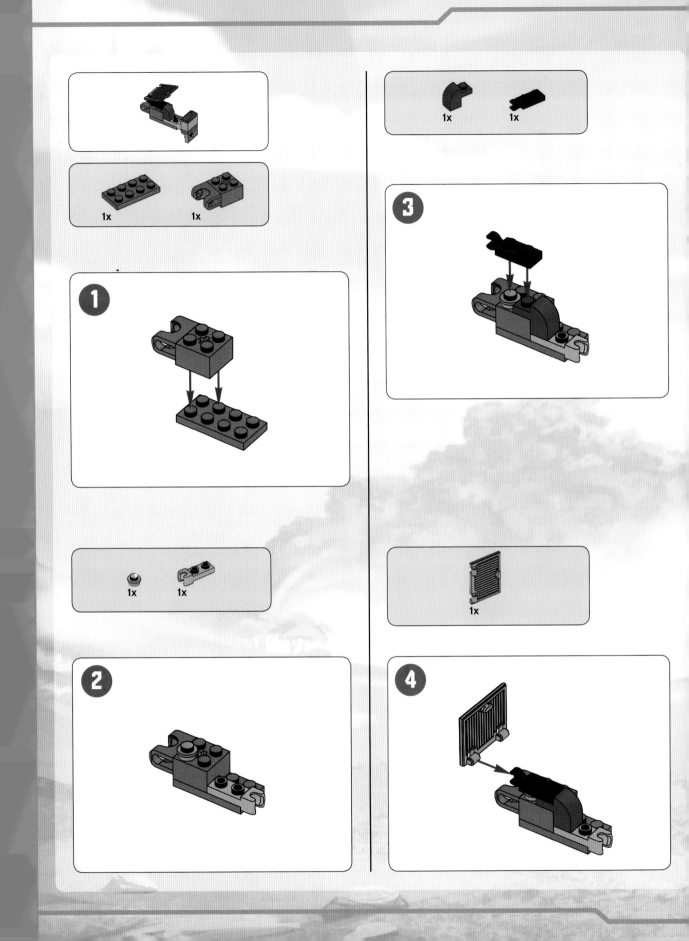

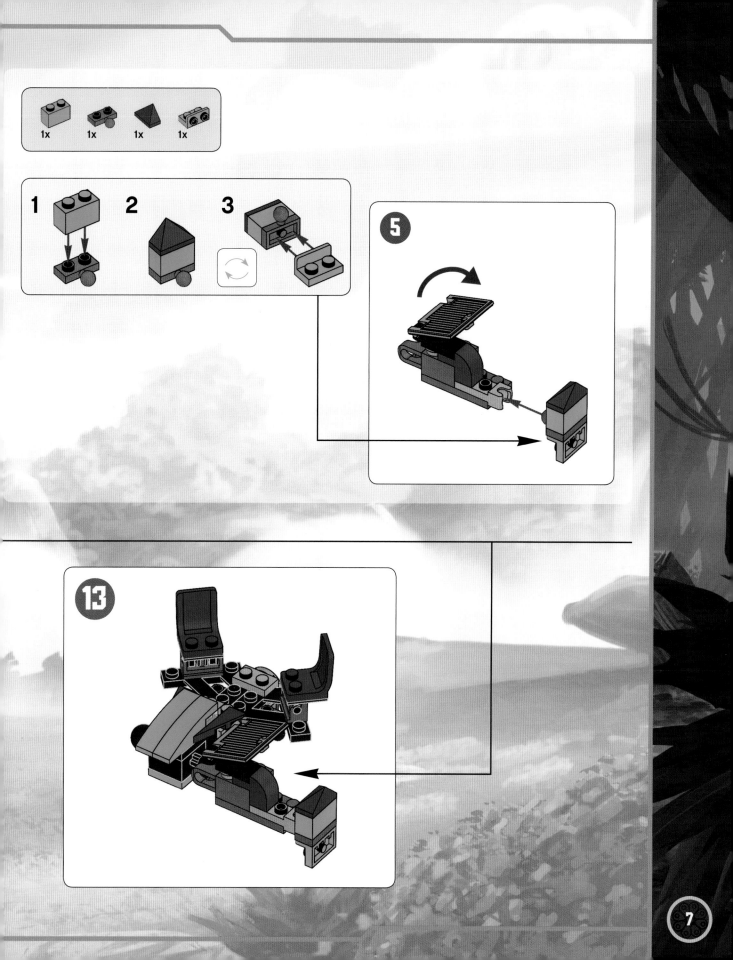

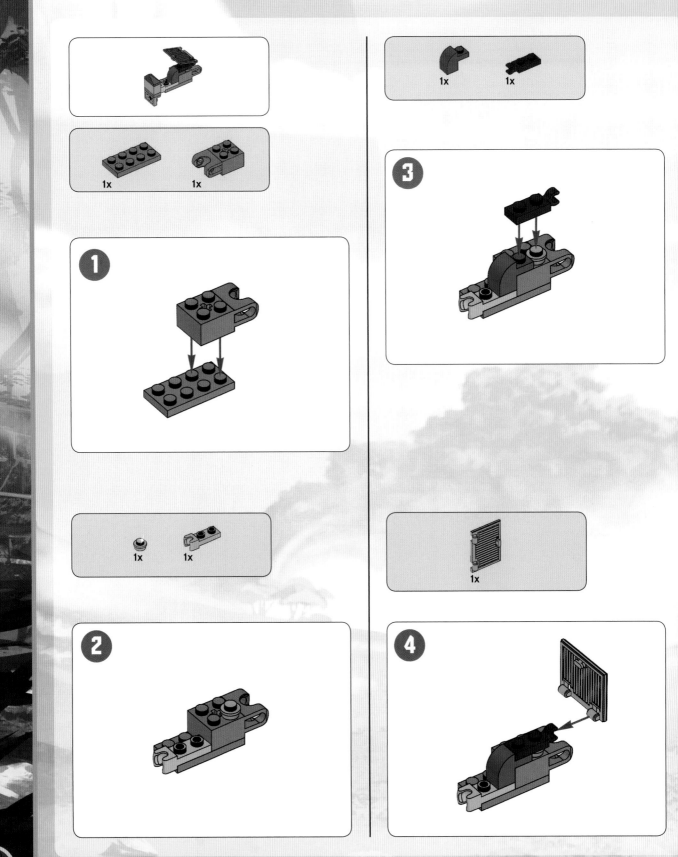

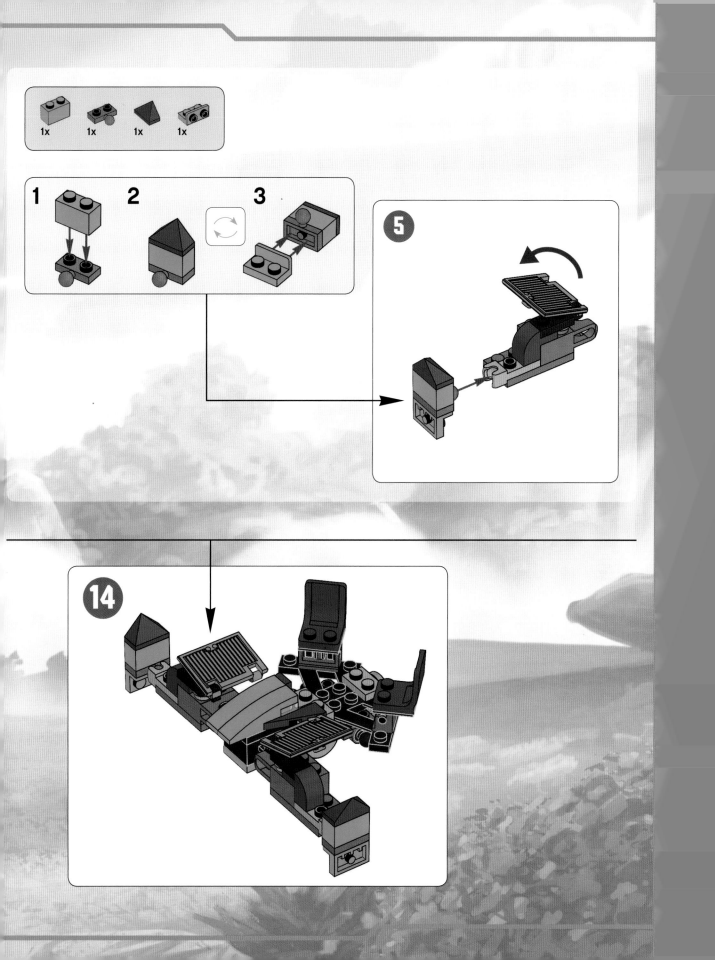

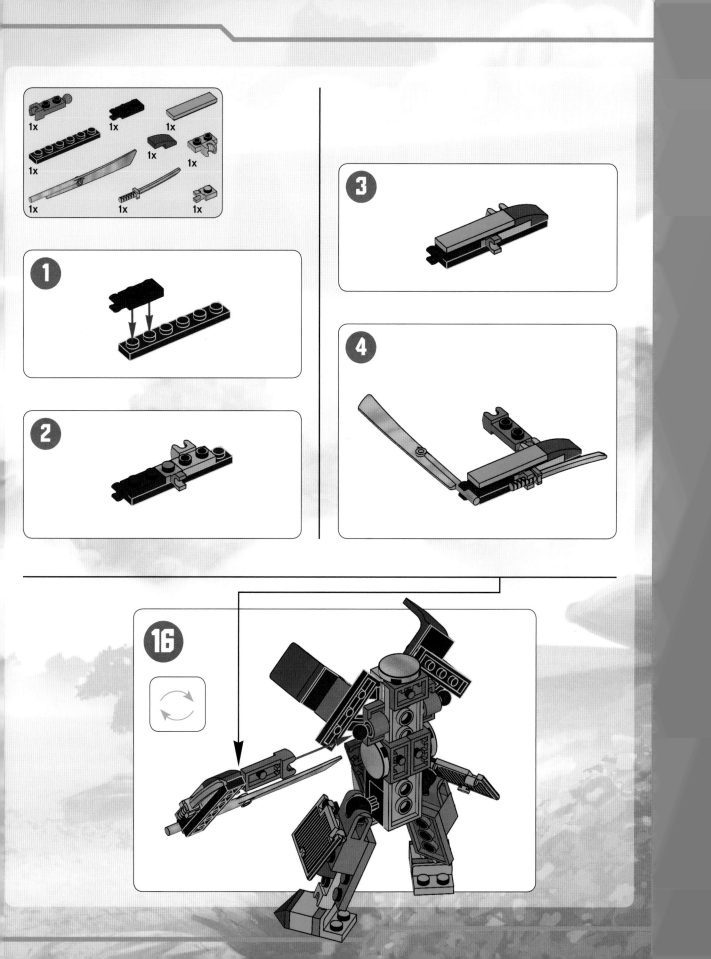

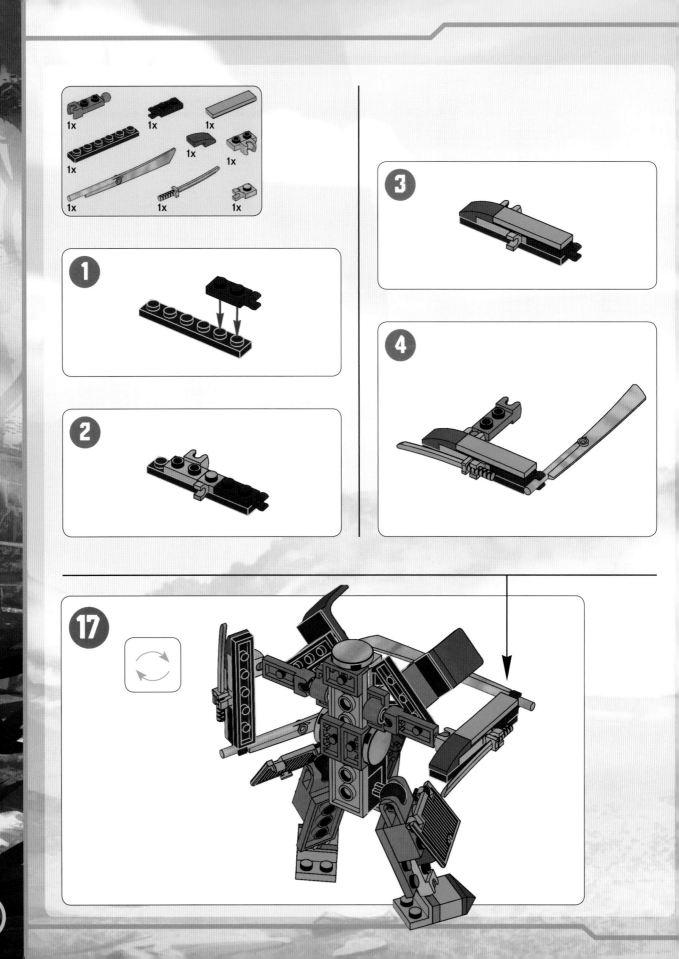

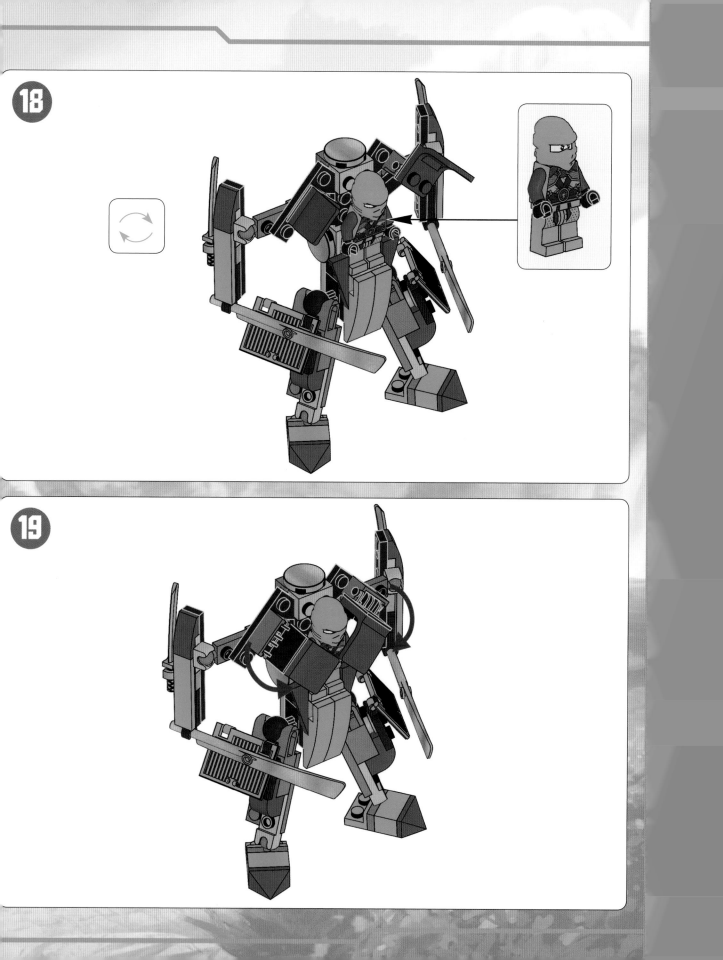

BUILDING YOUR OWN ADVENTURE

In the pages of this book, you will discover an exciting LEGO® NINJAGO® adventure story. You will also see some clever ideas for LEGO NINJAGO models that might inspire you to create your own. Building LEGO models from your own imagination is creative and endlessly fun. There are no limits to what you can build. This is your adventure, so jump right in and get building!

HOW TO USE THIS BOOK

This book will not show you how to build the models, because it's unlikely that you'll have exactly the same bricks in your own collection. It will show you some useful build tips and model breakdowns that will help you when it comes to building your own models. Here's how the pages work...

Sometimes, different views of the same model are shown

'What else will you build?' flashes give you even more ideas for models you could make

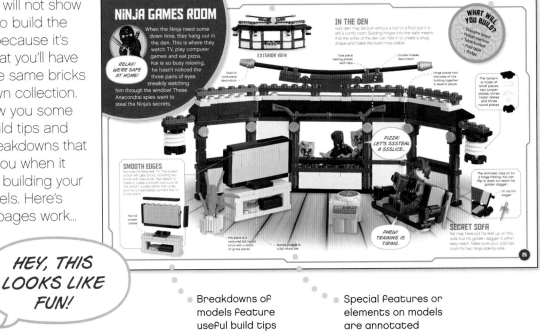

HEY, THIS LOOKS LIKE FUN!

Breakdowns of models feature useful build tips

Special features or elements on models are annotated

MEET THE BUILDER

Barney Main is a LEGO fan and super-builder, and he made all the inspirational LEGO models that can be found in this book. To make the models just right for the Ninjago world, Barney designed them alongside the LEGO NINJAGO team at the LEGO Group in Billund, Denmark. Use Barney's models to inspire your own LEGO NINJAGO models. Ninja Go!

BEFORE YOU BEGIN

Here are five handy hints to keep in mind every time you get out your bricks and prepare to build.

Organize your bricks
Organizing bricks into colors and types can save you time when you're building.

Make your model stable
Make a model that's sturdy enough to play with. You'll find useful tips for making a stable model in this book.

BUILD SOMETHING TO CATCH ME!

Be creative
If you don't have the perfect piece, find a creative solution! Look for a different piece that can create a similar effect.

Research
Look up pictures of what you want to build online or in books to inspire your ideas.

Have fun
Don't worry if your model goes wrong. Turn it into something else or start again. The fun is in the building!

BUILDER TALK

Did you know that LEGO® builders have their own language? You will find the terms below used a lot in this book. Here's what they all mean...

STUD

Round raised bumps on top of bricks and plates are called studs. A string has a single stud at each end. Studs fit into "tubes," which are on the bottom of bricks and plates.

2x2 corner plate

String with studs

MEASUREMENTS

Builders describe the size of LEGO pieces according to the number of studs on them. If a brick has 2 studs across and 3 up, it's a 2x3 brick. If a piece is tall, it has a third number that is its height in standard bricks.

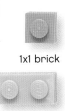

1x1 brick

1x2 brick

2x2 brick

2x3 brick

1x1x5 brick

CLIP

Some pieces have clips on them, into which you can fit other elements. Pieces such as ladders fasten onto bars using built-in clips.

1x1 plate with vertical clip

1x1 plate with horizontal clip

Flag with 2 clips

HOLE

Bricks and plates with holes are very useful. They will hold bars or LEGO® Technic pins or connectors.

1X1 brick with hole

2x3 curved plate with hole

2x2 round brick

1x2 brick with 2 holes

4x4 round brick

Ladder with 2 clips

SIDEWAYS BUILDING

Sometimes you need to build in two directions. That's when you need bricks or plates like these, with studs on more than one side.

1x4 brick with side studs

1x1 brick with 2 side studs

1x2/1x4 angle plate

1x1 brick with 1 side stud

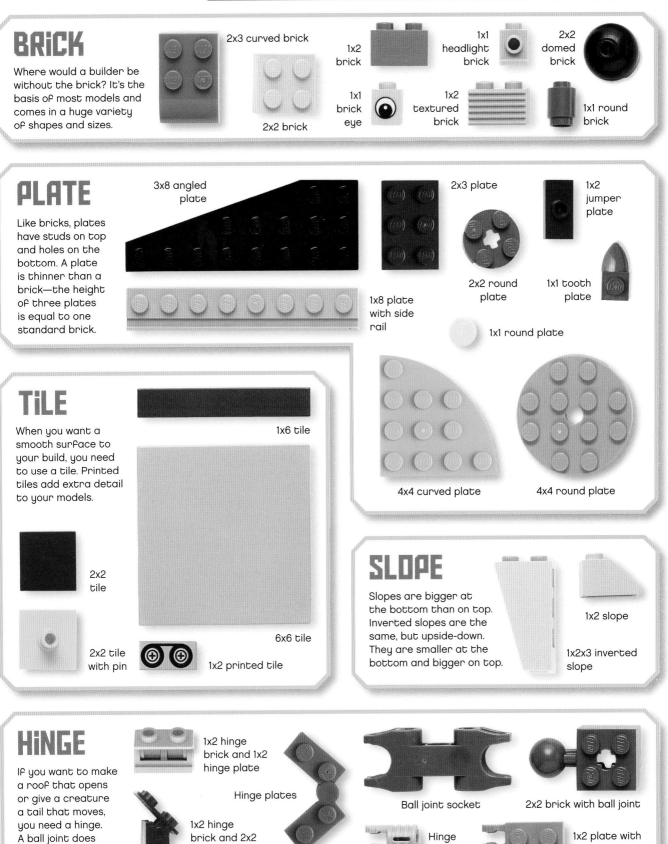

BRICK

Where would a builder be without the brick? It's the basis of most models and comes in a huge variety of shapes and sizes.

2x3 curved brick

2x2 brick

1x2 brick

1x1 headlight brick

2x2 domed brick

1x1 brick eye

1x2 textured brick

1x1 round brick

PLATE

Like bricks, plates have studs on top and holes on the bottom. A plate is thinner than a brick—the height of three plates is equal to one standard brick.

3x8 angled plate

2x3 plate

1x2 jumper plate

2x2 round plate

1x1 tooth plate

1x8 plate with side rail

1x1 round plate

4x4 curved plate

4x4 round plate

TILE

When you want a smooth surface to your build, you need to use a tile. Printed tiles add extra detail to your models.

1x6 tile

2x2 tile

2x2 tile with pin

6x6 tile

1x2 printed tile

SLOPE

Slopes are bigger at the bottom than on top. Inverted slopes are the same, but upside-down. They are smaller at the bottom and bigger on top.

1x2 slope

1x2x3 inverted slope

HINGE

If you want to make a roof that opens or give a creature a tail that moves, you need a hinge. A ball joint does the same job, too.

1x2 hinge brick and 1x2 hinge plate

Hinge plates

1x2 hinge brick and 2x2 hinge plate

Ball joint socket

2x2 brick with ball joint

Hinge cylinder

1x2 plate with click hinge

LLOYD

Lloyd is the Green Ninja. He is the youngest member of the team, but also the most powerful. He loves his new mech!

KAI

Kai is the most hotheaded Ninja, but he is learning to control his temper. As the Ninja of Fire, Kai is ablaze with energy.

JAY

Jay loves to joke around, but that doesn't get in the way of his Ninja training. He is the quick-thinking Ninja of Lightning.

COLE

The leader of the Ninja team, Cole is strong and reliable. He is the rock-solid Ninja of Earth.

NINJA GO!

Are you ready to go on a brilliant building adventure? Lloyd is ready and so is his shiny new Green Ninja Mech. So let's meet all the friends and foes who will play a part in our exciting story— from brave Ninja warriors to slithering snakes. It doesn't matter if you have different friends and foes in your LEGO NINJAGO collection. They are all welcome to join in, too!

ZANE

As the Ninja of Ice, Zane is always cool under pressure. He is a little different from the other Ninja, as he is really a robot!

HOME

The Ninja live in an ancient land with many different parts—some more welcoming than others! Four powerful Elements define this land: Fire, Ice, Earth, and Lightning. Four of the Ninja have skills that are linked to these Elements.

WU

Sensei Wu is a skilled Ninja Master. He has trained the five Ninja well and made them into an unstoppable force.

NYA

Nya is Kai's sister. She has proven herself to be just as brave as her Ninja brother and his teammates.

THE ANACONDRAI

A tribe of sinister snakes and their human henchmen, the Anacondrai are known for having the most powerful warriors in Ninjago history. They are out to cause trouble wherever they can!

TROUBLE IS BREWING...

The Anacondrai have heard about Lloyd's new mech, and are very jealous. They have come up with a plan to steal the blueprints for this mean machine so they can make their very own mech—snake-style!

MEDITATION ROOM

Welcome to the Ninja's home! There is lots of space for all the Ninja to hang out and do what they like to do. Sensei Wu and Zane love the meditation room on the first floor. They can relax here knowing that the entire house is protected by clever traps, designed to catch out any unwelcome visitors.

I LOVE CHILLING OUT WITH WU.

ENTRANCE

To enter the Ninja house, guests must walk up a drawbridge to a doorway guarded by a swinging ax. A gray radar dish covers the turning mechanism— a LEGO® Technic axle that runs through a brick with a hole. Turning the dish moves the ax from side to side.

Brown plates are layered with round bricks to create a wooden doorway

Steps built up using layers of plates and bricks

Bonsai plant has offset round plates as leaves, on top of a small pot.

Central brick with side studs

Banners made using radar dish plus Wu's hat and two swords

EXTERIOR VIEW

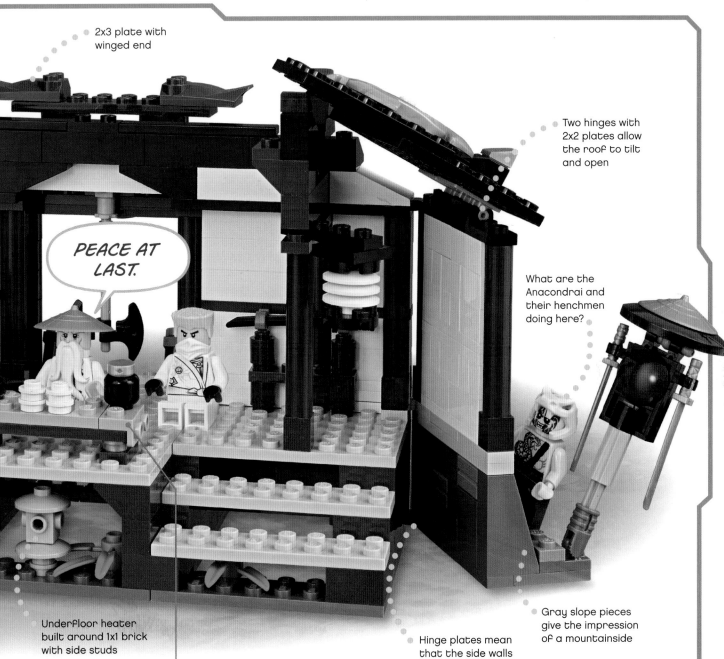

2x3 plate with winged end

Two hinges with 2x2 plates allow the roof to tilt and open

PEACE AT LAST.

What are the Anacondrai and their henchmen doing here?

Gray slope pieces give the impression of a mountainside

Underfloor heater built around 1x1 brick with side studs

Hinge plates mean that the side walls can open outwards

TABLE TOP

Wu's tea table has gold 1x1 round plates for legs and angle plates for a table cloth. It is set with two tea cups, a pan for hot water, and a round jar of tea. Each tea cup is two 1x1 round plates, a good alternative for a LEGO® mug piece.

Gold 1x1 round plate

FIRST FLOOR

This is the first floor of the Ninja's home. It is built directly into the mountaintop, with raised floorboards hiding a heater and the foundations below. The top of this level is designed with smooth tiles and jumper plates so that another floor can be easily added or removed.

NINJA GAME ROOM

When the Ninja need some down time, they hang out in the den. This is where they watch TV, play computer games, and eat pizza. Kai is so busy relaxing, he hasn't noticed the three pairs of eyes sneakily watching him through the window! These Anacondrai spies want to steal the Ninja's secrets.

RELAX! WE'RE SAFE AT HOME!

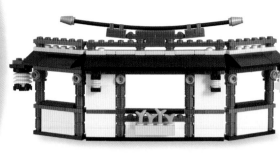

EXTERIOR VIEW

Gold 1x1 cone piece decoration

SMOOTH EDGES

Kai loves his flatscreen TV. The screen is built with gray bricks, including two bricks with side studs. Tiles attach to these to create a smooth surround. At the bottom, a plate, rather than a tile, and two jumper plates connect the TV to the stand.

Two 1x2 jumper plates

Pot plant is a textured 2x2 round brick with a stack of grass pieces

Games console is a 2x2 round tile

IN THE DEN

Kai's den may be built without a roof or a floor, but it is still a comfy room. Building hinges into the walls means that the sides of the den can fold in to create a snug shape and make the build more stable.

WHAT WILL YOU BUILD?

- Checkers board
- Pinball machine
- Table football
- Pool table
- Fridge

Tube piece held by plates with clips

Double musket decoration

Hinge plates hold the sides of the building together in several places

The lantern is made of small pieces: two jumper plates, three radar dishes, and three round plates.

PIZZA! LET'S SSSTEAL A SSSLICE...

The armrest clips on to a hinge fitting. Kai can flip it down to reach his golden dagger.

1X1 clip for dagger

PHEW! TRAINING IS TIRING.

SECRET SOFA

Kai may have put his feet up on this sofa, but his golden dagger is within easy reach. Make sure your sofa has room for two Ninja side-by-side.

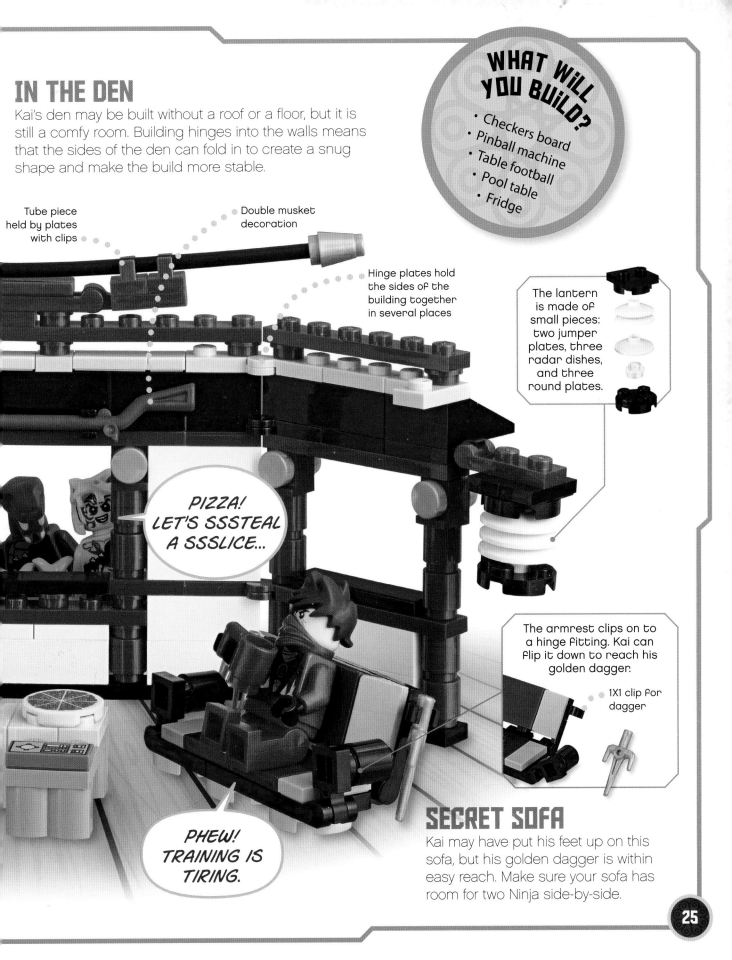

OUTDOOR TRAINING

Cole likes to be super-fit, so he has built a training course outside the Ninja's house. It tests his strength, agility, and reflexes—everything a Ninja needs to fight his enemies. One of the Anacondrai has been sent to spy on Cole, but when he sees how strong and skilled the Ninja is, he quickly slithers away!

I'M FEELING PRETTY EPIC RIGHT NOW!

THIS NINJA HAS SSOME SSERIOUS SSSKILLS.

SWING GYM

In Cole's outdoor gym, three sturdy red towers are linked by two tough crossings. First, a tube piece, held firmly in place by plates with clips, supports three chain swings. Then, two ladder pieces are connected to make challenging monkey bars. Don't look down, Cole!

Short chain attached to the back of a plate with clip

A 1x1 plate with clip holds the tube piece at both ends

An uneven surface, made with overlapping plates, is more of a challenge for Cole!

2x2 round plate

Textured 2x2 round brick

Smooth tiles in the middle attach to bricks with side studs.

1x1 brick with two side studs

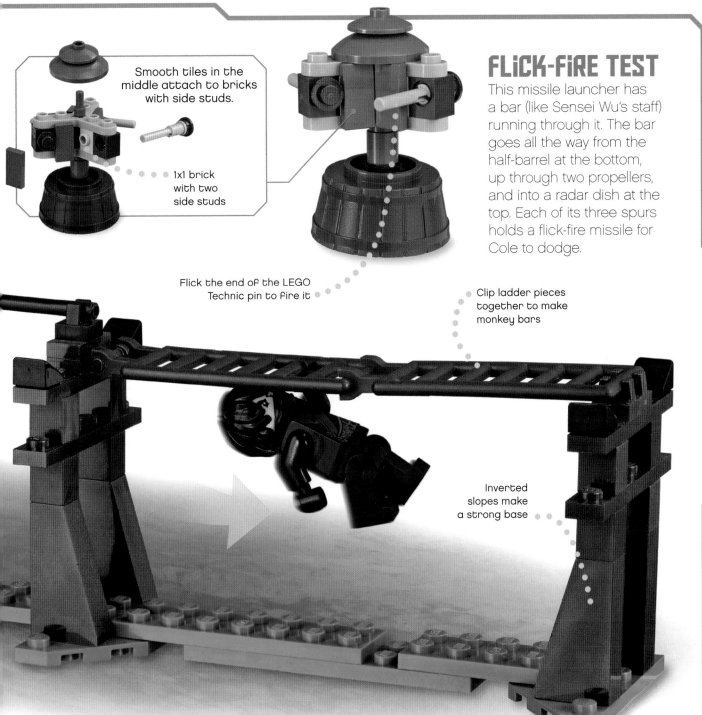

FLICK-FIRE TEST

This missile launcher has a bar (like Sensei Wu's staff) running through it. The bar goes all the way from the half-barrel at the bottom, up through two propellers, and into a radar dish at the top. Each of its three spurs holds a flick-fire missile for Cole to dodge.

Flick the end of the LEGO Technic pin to fire it

Clip ladder pieces together to make monkey bars

Inverted slopes make a strong base

1x1 round bricks make a good bar for Cole to break

1x1 slopes hold bar in place

TRAINING GEAR

You only need a few basic pieces to make training gear. These balance beams, stepping towers, and breaking bar with blocks are all made with small bricks and plates. Vary the size and shapes of the obstacles, depending on what is in your collection.

NYA'S WORKSHOP

Nya has a cool workshop in the basement of the Ninja's house. She has just finished building something there—an amazing Green Ninja Mech for Lloyd. He loves it! The pair decide to lock the blueprints away where they can't be stolen. But just as Lloyd is printing them out, they are distracted by a sound...

MINE IS THE GREATEST MECH EVER!

WALLS AND SHELVES

Two solid walls connected with hinge plates create a great workshop for the Ninja. Build in a shelf and a TV monitor so that they form part of the walls. Then use small pieces to make jars and tins to fill the shelves.

Tile gives a smooth edge

This bottle is made from a faucet piece and a round brick

WORKBENCH

Nya's workbench is always tidy! It has a drawer that slides in and out, and a handy vice made from 1x2 rail plates and a joystick element. On the other side, there is a row of tools.

Plates with clips hold tools

HEY! DID YOU HEAR SOMETHING?

Put smooth tiles under the drawer so it slides in and out easily.

1x4 tile

This shelf is held up with two inverted slope bricks built into the wall.

SCREEN FIX

Use some clever building techniques to fix the TV screen to the wall. It looks as though it is hanging on the wall but most of the white bricks are built directly into the wall. This makes it a strong build.

String with studs connects welding torch to gas canister

Pressure gauge

You could add a stripe to the gas canister

WHAT WILL YOU BUILD?
- Weapons testing area
- Car mechanic's lift
- Laboratory bench
- Mech prototypes
- Laptop

Joystick pieces are the TV aerial

Drill bit is actually a screwdriver

EQUIPMENT

Fill your workshop with smaller equipment such as this welding torch and drill press. Small accessories, including a screwdriver and steering wheel, have been used to make the drill press.

PRINTER

Curved bricks give this printer its smooth edges. A plain white tile acts as the paper going in, and a printed tile makes the finished mech blueprints. Let's hope they don't get forgotten about!

Warning light is a transparent red slope

Try colored tiles, if you haven't got printed ones

String with studs makes printer wires

HOUSE OF NINJA

The Anacondrai have stolen the plans for the Green Ninja Mech! They distracted Lloyd and Nya, then seized their chance while the other Ninja relaxed. Jay rushes from the bathroom and joins the others just in time to see the snakes slithering away. The Ninja agree that they must get the plans back, no matter what!

THEY WON'T GET AWAY WITH IT...

EXTERIOR VIEW

Golden spinner makes a cool detail

Rows of sloped bricks forms a solid foundation

NINJA BASE

The meditation room and the game room make the first two floors of the Ninja house. A bathroom fits on top. If you want to stack your builds like this, it is best to fix each room to strong interior pillars and walls in the one below.

Banner is angled on a hinge cylinder

DO YOU MIND? I'M TAKING A BATH HERE!

Flag piece clipped to bar forms a towel

1x1 round brick is a toilet roll

Curved half arches for the bathtub

Two slopes, a 1x2 plate, and a headlight brick make this rubber duck!

BATHROOM

When you build a bathroom, make sure the bath can accommodate a minifigure. The hinged roof opens for easy access to the inside, though right now Jay would like some privacy, please!

WHAT WILL YOU BUILD?

- Kitchen and dining area
- Top-floor lookout post
- Ninja bedrooms
- Zen garden
- Garage

INTERIOR
VIEW

ROOF OPENING

Each side of this roof lifts open thanks to two pairs of 2x2 hinge plates. Golden swords and slope pieces are the finishing touches.

This is the game room from pages 24-25

This is the meditation room from pages 22-23

HEY! BRING THOSE BACK!

TOO SSSLOW, NINJA!

JUNGLE CAMP

The Ninja waste no time before setting off in pursuit of the sneaky Anacondrai that have stolen their Green Ninja Mech blueprints. Jay thinks the snakes will head for the jungle, and so he, Cole, Kai, Zane, Lloyd, and Nya pack up all the equipment they will need and make their way into the wild...

JUNGLE HERE WE COME!

Lamp fixed with a holder piece

LANTERN

It's dark in the jungle! The Ninja will need a powerful lantern to light their camp. This one is made using a 1x1 brick with side studs covered with 1x1 round tiles, with 2x2 radar dishes at the top and bottom.

This 4x4 curved plate is a steady base

Hat with 1x1 round brick beneath decorates tent

Sides of tent rest on central pillar of round bricks and plates

Hinge bricks enable sides to open and tilt

TENTS ARE INTENSE!

NINJA TENT

The Ninja also need a place to sleep in the jungle, so Jay quickly puts a tent together. Begin with a strong frame then add hinges for the sides. Don't forget to make it big enough for a minifigure!

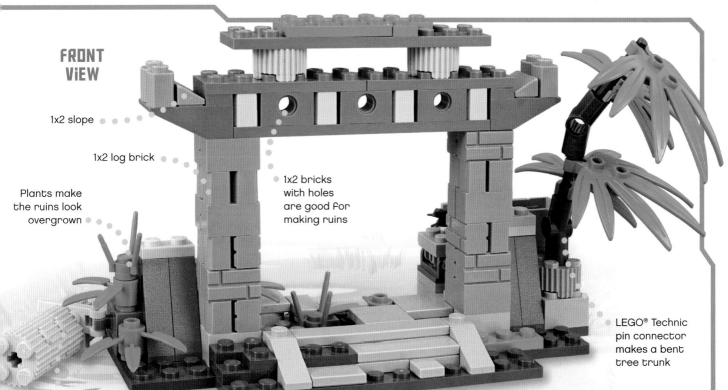

FRONT VIEW

1x2 slope

1x2 log brick

Plants make the ruins look overgrown

1x2 bricks with holes are good for making ruins

LEGO® Technic pin connector makes a bent tree trunk

This fallen pillar is actually clipped on to the main build.

SLIDE TRAP

This hinged box can be used to slide snakes onto unsuspecting Ninja. Edge plates on a 2x6 plate make a box that is open at one end. A hinge brick underneath the open end allows it to tip out its contents. A 2x2 tile under the other end of the box supports it when it is not tipped up.

SNAKE RUINS

There are ruins from an ancient civilisation in this jungle. Ruins are fun to build because they don't need to be perfect—they should look ruined! These ruins hide a scary secret—a trap full of snakes!

WHAT WILL YOU BUILD?

- Brightly colored birds
- Giant jungle scorpion
- Treetop walkway
- Ruined village
- Campfire

REAR VIEW

Pillar hinges on 1x2 plate with bar fixed to 1x1 plate with clip

SWAMP ATTACK

Jay was right: the Anacondrai are in the jungle! Cole spots one of their henchmen on patrol in a special swamp craft. Jay is quick to give chase in his super-fast speeder, but this steamy swamp is not an easy place to navigate. Can the Ninja of Lightning make his way through all its obstacles and traps?

THIS LOOKS LIKE A JOB FOR JAY...

SCARY HEAD

The head of the craft can rear up on clip hinges to frighten the Anacondrai's foes. Its front fangs slot into 1x1 plates with side rings, fastened to an angle plate. The smaller teeth, made from horn pieces, slot into plates with clips.

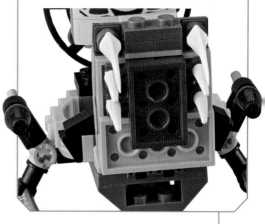

SWAMP CRAFT

This reptilian fan boat flies across the surface of the swamp on wide waterski blades. Both blades are attached to LEGO Technic angled connectors, as are two flick-fire missile launchers. There are fierce fangs at the front, and a powerful propeller at the back.

LEGO Technic pin allows propeller to spin

Flick-fire missile in launcher

LEGO Technic angled connector

Long blade doubles as waterski

Windshield is a transparent edge plate

Round plate and round tile make this evil eye

1x1 plate with side ring holds tooth

Two 1x10 curved bricks

JAY'S SPEEDER

Skimming the swamp at high speed, Jay's craft is equipped with a huge engine and flick-fire missiles. The missiles fit into 1x2 plates with rings on top, hidden under the wings.

Engine slots on to LEGO Technic pin

This 1x6 plate has a 1x1 slope where it touches the bottom section

Top leaf section balances on this 1x4 plate

Front section built sideways on angle plate

The wings fit onto hinges built sideways from angle plates.

Long LEGO Technic pin

Two bricks stop lower leaf tilting back too far

PLANT TRAP

Look out! The Anacondrai have set a trap to catch Jay. If his speeder presses down on the bottom leaf, the whole thing snaps shut like hungry jaws!

Tiles and plates hold the leaves in place and secure half arch to slope brick

Build the left and right sides separately

LEGO Technic lever

The two sides of the foliage tilt on LEGO Technic axles, running through 2x2 plates with rings underneath. A LEGO Technic angled connector is the lever that separates them.

SECRET ESCAPE

Things are not what they seem in this jungle. These plants look too thick to get through, but pressing on the LEGO Technic angled connector opens up a secret pathway. The Anacondrai use it to escape!

OBSTACLE COURSE

As Jay gets further into the swamp, he finds even more obstacles blocking his way. Leaving his speeder, he must use his own lightning-fast skills to dodge the traps the Anacondrai have set for him. The other Ninja can only watch from the edge of the swamp—but there are dangers there, too!

THIS SWAMP IS BOGGING US DOWN!

Flame piece fits into the bottom of the barrel

2x2 slide plate has curved bottom

FIRE BARRELS

A row of fiery barrels blocks Jay's path. Each one has a curved 2x2 slide plate on its base, making them wobbly and unpredictable obstacles.

Skull is topped with a radar dish and flame element

Spooky skeleton head is a warning to trespassers

Dirt mound made from slope pieces

ENJOY THE TRIP, NINJA!

SWAMP

Curved plates makes a good base for this swampy scenery. Two 4x6 curved bricks make the main mound, with differently sized pieces on top to create a natural, overgrown look.

Transparent green slopes glisten like swamp gunk

4x4 curved plates make a good base for a swamp

Transparent plates look like swampy sludge

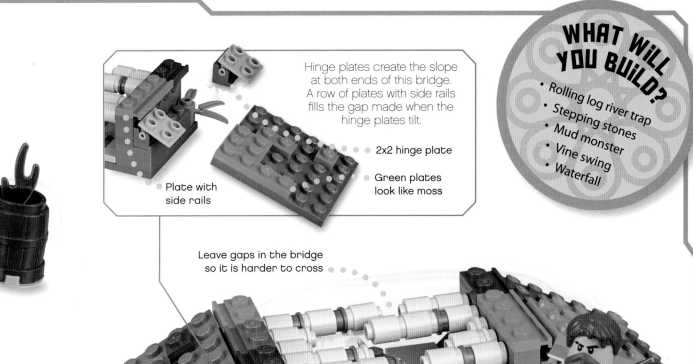

Hinge plates create the slope at both ends of this bridge. A row of plates with side rails fills the gap made when the hinge plates tilt.

Plate with side rails

2x2 hinge plate

Green plates look like moss

WHAT WILL YOU BUILD?
- Rolling log river trap
- Stepping stones
- Mud monster
- Vine swing
- Waterfall

Leave gaps in the bridge so it is harder to cross

Horn and green 2x2 round plate makes a lily pad

BAMBOO BRIDGE

Jay must cross this rickety bridge to catch up with the Anacondrai. The 1x1 round bricks that make up its span can turn on LEGO Technic pins fitted into bricks with holes, making it super slippery!

1x1 round plates look like mold or weeds

TRIP WIRE

At the edge of the swamp, Kai spots this trip wire just in time to avoid falling in. It is made from two tube elements, held in place at each end by 1x1 plates with vertical clips.

Two 1x1 plates with clips hold the tube firm

JUNGLE CHASE

THESE SNAKES ARE ON WHEELS!

Jay meets the other Ninja on the far side of the swamp, but the slippery Anacondrai are nowhere to be seen. Lloyd is the first to spot some tire tracks leading off between the trees. It looks like the snakes have got a car to help them get away! Lucky that Jay has a mighty 4x4 to carry on the chase...

CAR BASICS

Master the basics of this car, and you'll have a good starting point for your own creations. A 2x6 plate is a good base for a small car. Add a 2x2 axle plate with wheels at both ends and some plates with clips near the middle, then fix it all in place with another 2x6 plate on top. Give the wheels a test-spin before you carry on building.

2x6 top plate

2x2 axle plate

BRRMMM!

Fang attaches to plate with clip and builds up side of vehicle

Bony bumper attaches to two plates with clips

Tail piece attached to skeleton torso

Skeleton torso fits on to plate with horizontal clips

Rocky slope piece provides tough armor for the car

REAR VIEW

1x1 round plates suggest engine

Fang slots in to headlight brick

SNAKE CAR

Only the Anacondrai would have a vehicle like this! It has fangs at the front and a long tail at the back. To make it extra scary, it's covered in bones, too!

Protective cage built on to a row on plates with clips

Front section built sideways onto hidden angle plates

Cannon made from four LEGO Technic pin connectors

2x2 turntable under 4x4 round plate enables cannon to rotate

Transparent blue bar slots into LEGO Technic connector

Weapon fitted at right angles using LEGO Technic connectors

Blaster made from binoculars attached to 1x1 plate with clip

REAR VIEW

JAY'S 4X4

Huge LEGO Technic wheels carry Jay deep into snake territory. His monster 4x4 is built using a similar basic chassis to the snake car, but on a much larger scale. It also has some cool extra features, such as a spinning blaster cannon on the front and extra weapons on both sides. Golden curved bricks give the vehicle its streamlined shape.

Front and back wheels thread onto LEGO Technic cross axles

TREEHOUSE ASSAULT

Jay and the other Ninja have traced the Anacondrai to their jungle hideout. The snakes have made their base in an impressive treehouse and are ready to start work on their own mech. The Ninja need to get their blueprints back before it's too late—but can they get past the snakes' defenses?

IT'S TIME TO RUMBLE IN THE JUNGLE!

I'M WASTING AWAY...

LEGO Technic pieces support the chain

Ladder tops fit into plates with clips

CAGE

To show that the Anacondrai mean business, this Ninja-sized cage dangles from their jungle base. It is hanging from a long chain that attaches to a round 2x2 plate that has plates with clips underneath. Whoever is inside looks like he's been there for quite some time!

BREAK OUT

Four ladder pieces with clips fasten onto four 1x2 plates with handled bars to make the sides of the cage. The plates with bars are held in place between two 2x4 plates and a 4X4 round plate. This makes a strong base for the cage.

4x4 round plate

Plate with handled bar

REAR VIEW

GET BACK IN YOUR TREE, SNAKE!

HISSSSS!

Coffee machine

Crane rotates on 2x2 turntable

A large barrel on top of a stack of round bricks makes a good lookout

Half arches and inverted half arches create this circular entrance

TREEHOUSE

This treetop lair is the perfect place for the Anacondrai to keep watch for any approaching Ninja! As well as a crow's nest lookout and a scary prison cell, it also has a crane for winching supplies up from the jungle floor, and a rotating weapons rack. Inside, the snakes have even found room for some flowers and a coffee machine. Every hideout needs that extra homely touch!

Roof can open up thanks to hidden hinge elements on either side

Headlight brick, faucet, and transparent round brick make a lantern

Crane angles on hinge cylinder

Chain fits to 2x2 round plate on barrel

Large leaf elements help to camouflage treehouse

Column of round bricks made stronger with a LEGO Technic axle through its center

Be careful not to build your treehouse too tall—it might become unstable. Arches and half arches help to spread the weight of this treehouse across three sturdy columns of 2x2 round bricks.

Weapons rack can rotate on 2x2 turntable

TIME FOR LUNCH, BUDDY?

CHAPTER 3
GOING UNDERGROUND

ENTER THE CAVE

The Anacondrai gave the Ninja the slip in the jungle, and have slithered away with the stolen plans once more! Cole suspects they have gone underground and tracks them to a spooky cave. The Ninja don't hesitate to follow, but they should be wary. There are all kinds of traps waiting for them in the dark!

I'M READY FOR ANYTHING!

CAVE ENTRANCE

Caves need odd angles and uneven surfaces to look realistic. If you don't have any ready-made rock elements, try using slopes and inverted slopes in unusual arrangements. This cave was once a busy gold mine, but has now been abandoned. It has a grand entrance with sloping sides, but has become overgrown with moss.

These plates attach sideways onto the wall

Green plates are like moss covering the top of the entrance

Top of entrance built from two curved "macaroni" bricks

Use plates with clips to fix these drips of venom to the back of the model. Try setting them at different heights to make the model more realistic.

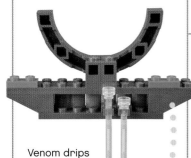

Venom drips slowly to the ground

Inverted slope supports the roof of the entrance

Angled pillar held in place with hinges at top and bottom

Transparent 1x2 plates look like pools of venom

To build a wobbly ledge for the Ninja to cross, build a brick with a hole into your wall. Then use a LEGO® Technic pin to attach a plate with a ring underneath. A 2x6 plate fits on top to complete your unstable platform.

LEGO Technic pin

Transparent aerial piece drips venom onto the cave floor

Bats hang from 1x1 bricks with handles

The Ninja will need to grab this short chain so they can swing from ledge to ledge

Low entrance made from four 1x1 bricks with a 1x8 plate and tile on top

CAVE WALL

The wall of the cave is filled with lots of hazards such as narrow ledges and drips of venom. If you want to add features like this to a model, plan your build out first—it's much easier than trying to add details later.

Pool of venom is radar dish on 1x1 round plate

Different-sized cones look like stalagmites

Scary red spider lurks in the dark

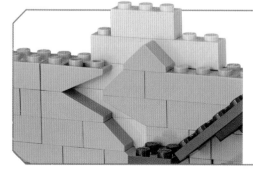

CRACK IN THE WALL

To include a crack effect in your wall, use a double layer of bricks. If possible, use a different color for the bricks behind. The front layer includes sloped bricks that reveal the bricks behind. You need only use a different color for the bricks in the area behind the crack.

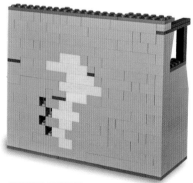

REAR VIEW

CAVE HAZARDS

Deep in the cave, the Ninja find a pair of lanterns. When they light them, they see a glinting pair of fangs! But this is not an animal—it's a digging machine. It looks like the Anacondrai are making an underground base. The Ninja follow an Anacondrai worker to see where he goes. Will they spot the rockfall trap in time?

LANTERNS ARE A BRIGHT IDEA!

LANTERNS

Cole and Kai find some lanterns to light their way. These are built with radar dishes and transparent bricks, but you could use round plates or tiles to make the lantern frame. Try using orange or yellow pieces to create a glowing lamp.

Wrench element is inserted into a radar dish

Transparent 1x1 round brick

The digger's cog wheels are attached with two LEGO Technic pins. A 2x2 plate with rings underneath holds the two pins in place.

1x2 plate with rings underneath

LAMP PARTS

To make a lantern, start with a 1x1 brick with side studs. Attach transparent plates or tiles on four sides of the brick, then fix radar dishes above and below. The wrench piece at the top of the lamp holds the top radar dish in place.

Fangs attached to plates with clips give the digger a snake-like look

I LIKE TO HISS WHILE I WORK.

HAND DiGGER

The Ninja spy an Anacondrai worker making tunnels with this hand digger. It has cog wheels for tearing through the earth and a 1x2 plate with handles so a minifigure can hold on to it.

1x2 plate with bar

Barred fence holds rocks in place

Flags with clips make these sides

Platform fits neatly into the ceiling

Girder adds an industrial look

ROCKFALL TRAP

This wooden structure has a secret in its roof. The platform on top holds a collection of bricks ready to drop onto any victims below. The floor of the platform slides out to release the bricks.

1x6 gray tile locks together the pieces below

Tile with clips holds the bone handle

WORKING TRAP

For a working rockfall trap, build a four-sided structure with an open top and add smooth tiles for a platform to slide in and out on. Build a separate platform to fit on top and cover this with tiles, too. Add bricks or plates to the top of the structure to hold the rocks (loose round bricks), and to keep the sliding platform in place.

A mix of tile sizes covers the platform

Instead of pillars, your Ninja trap could have archways, doors, or even walls with spikes

What else could you drop onto your foes—snakes, spiders, or bones, maybe?

UNDERGROUND MINE

There is lots of old mining equipment this far inside the cave. The Ninja find tools and rusty mining carts that must have been left there a long time ago. It looks as if they have reached a dead end, but then Jay spots some old explosives and a detonator. Cole blasts through the wall to see what's on the other side...

THIS IS SURE TO BE A BLAST.

MINING CART

Each mining cart is built up from a 2x6 plate. The sides of the wagons have click hinges for loading and unloading, and two sets of small train wheels as if they were designed to run on tracks.

The carts are linked by a short chain that wraps around a bar.

Smooth tiles on the top

Click hinge

Small train wheel

IT'S NOT THE CART RATTLING, IT'S ME!

1x6x5 girder element

Brown pieces look like rust

Holder fits between a 1x2 textured brick and a 1x4 tile

Inverted slopes at both ends of the cart give it its shape. Hatch pieces with hinges form the sloping sides and can fold down for unloading.

2x6 plate

Pickax

Shovel

EQUIPMENT RACK

This mine is full of vicious-looking tools. No wonder the Anacondrai like it here! Any tool a minifigure can hold will fit on to these holder elements. What tools will you make to go on your rack?

3... 2... 1... FIRE!

Danger: explosives!

WHAT WILL YOU BUILD?

- Mine elevator and shaft
- Conveyor belt to surface
- Giant tunneling drill
- Rock crusher
- Digger

Rock wall piece is ready to be blown away

String with studs

2x2 turntable

1x8 tile

Fit a bar onto a turntable behind the wall. Make sure the bar is long enough to hit the cave wall when turned.

Gold deposits in the rock

Round plate at end of bar knocks into rock piece

Dynamite is two round bricks

Detonator box is a log brick

Cave wall is a single rock piece

EXPLODING WALL

This rocky wall looks solid at first, but the front section only rests on tiles, and isn't built in. This means it falls away with a flick of a long bar attached to a turntable at the back of the model. Strike the bar as Cole sets off his powerful explosives.

ANCIENT TOMB

On the other side of the cave wall, the Ninja are amazed to find a huge cavern filled with treasure. At its center is a giant stone samurai head, and the dusty floor is littered with ancient bones. Lloyd trips up a snake skeleton and reaches out to grab a rock. The rock moves and the samurai head begins to open!

THIS GUY HAS A REALLY BIG HEAD!

FLAMING TORCHES

These flaming torches are easy to build, and add a spooky atmosphere to any scene. Set a flame into a brick with side studs, then fit this on its side into an upside-down radar dish. This attaches to an upside-down cone, which stands in a dish base.

Up-ended dish piece

SPINY SKELETON

The light from the flaming torches reveals a scary sight—an enormous snake skeleton lying in the dirt! Even though it's been dead for a very long time, it still looks pretty terrifying. Tooth plates make spikes along its back, and horn elements create fangs in its jaws.

HISS!

Plate with click hinge

HEAD BONES

Headlight bricks, set side by side, make excellent eyes for your creatures. Fit the headlight bricks into a 1x2 click hinge to create a jaw that can open and close.

Headlight brick

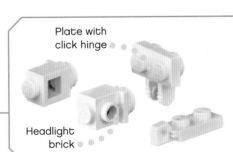

Plate with vertical clip

SAMURAI HEAD

This gigantic samurai head opens up to reveal its treasure—a special golden sword! A large build needs a solid base, such as these two curved slope plates. Wedge bricks and curved slopes create the face, complete with eyes and teeth!

Dome quarters make the top of the head

Golden katana blade

LIFTING THE HEAD

Two long LEGO Technic bricks are built in to the back of the samurai head to make a lever. The lever pivots on a LEGO Technic axle, so that the samurai's head lifts when the back of the lever is pressed. An inverted slope under the bar stops it from tilting too far.

LEGO Technic brick with holes

Large curved slope plates help to balance the head

Head is built in two sections so the mouth can open

1x1 round plates make the teeth

Lower jaw built in to base

Radar dish and ball joint makes giant eye

Two golden serpents protect the golden sword

HE JUST CAN'T KEEP HIS MOUTH SHUT!

53

BATTLE IN THE CAVE

The Anacondrai burst into the cavern eager to get their hands on the treasure that the Ninja have found. They haven't come alone, either—they have tamed a huge rocky snake that lives in these dark depths. Even worse, the mech plans are nowhere to be seen! Only Cole's saw-mobile can get the Ninja out of this...

YOU WANNA ROCK? I SAY WE ROLL!

LEGO Technic pin

LEGO Technic angled connector

LEGO Technic pins connect LEGO Technic angled connectors to the front of the vehicle. Two more pins connect these to the saw blades.

Cockpit built on 4x8 plate

Engine fan piece

Chunky wheels can easily ride over rocks

Saw-toothed blades tear through earth

REAR VIEW

Katana sword fixed to plate with clips

SAW-MOBILE

This tough, all-terrain vehicle has two monster saw blades and two chunky wheels. Its high front means Cole can smash through cave walls without getting hit with debris. The saw-mobile is built from some of the larger Ninjago parts. See what large parts you have, then try putting them together in new ways.

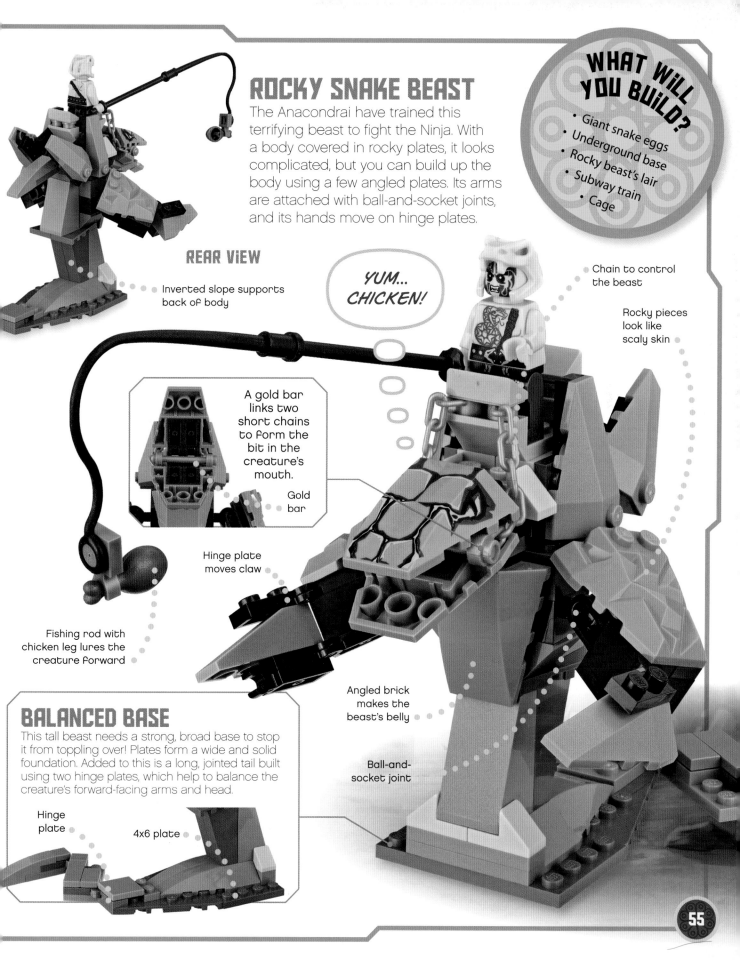

ROCKY SNAKE BEAST

The Anacondrai have trained this terrifying beast to fight the Ninja. With a body covered in rocky plates, it looks complicated, but you can build up the body using a few angled plates. Its arms are attached with ball-and-socket joints, and its hands move on hinge plates.

WHAT WILL YOU BUILD?
- Giant snake eggs
- Underground base
- Rocky beast's lair
- Subway train
- Cage

REAR VIEW

Inverted slope supports back of body

YUM... CHICKEN!

Chain to control the beast

Rocky pieces look like scaly skin

A gold bar links two short chains to form the bit in the creature's mouth.

Gold bar

Hinge plate moves claw

Fishing rod with chicken leg lures the creature forward

Angled brick makes the beast's belly

Ball-and-socket joint

BALANCED BASE

This tall beast needs a strong, broad base to stop it from toppling over! Plates form a wide and solid foundation. Added to this is a long, jointed tail built using two hinge plates, which help to balance the creature's forward-facing arms and head.

Hinge plate

4x6 plate

COME BACK! I ONLY LIKE TO TOAST MARSHMALLOWS!

ABANDONED VILLAGE

The Anacondrai escaped the caves and slithered away towards a fiery volcano. The Ninja give chase, crossing a bridge into a village at the foot of the volcano. Kai and Nya are the first to notice something is wrong. There's no one there! All the villagers must have run away to escape the relentless lava flow.

HEY! WHERE IS EVERYONE?

RICKSHAW

This rickshaw has been left empty in the street. Be sure to leave room for a seated minifigure inside, and add a harness element so that another minifigure can pull it along.

Harness element for the handles

The roof is a car hood piece with long bars fixed by plates with clips to its underside.

Small carriage wheels attach to bearing plate

BRIDGE STEPS

Each step of the bridge is made up of one plate with vertical clips and one plate with a bar. A rounded slide plate goes underneath and a jumper plate on top. The segments clip together to make a strong but flexible bridge crossing.

Jumper plate

1x2 plate with bar

Slide plate

1x2 plate with clips

LAVA BRIDGE

This rickety-looking lava bridge is actually a sturdy build. The segments connect to the supports at each end with clips and bars. The supports are made of sloped bricks, with a plate across the top.

Cone and tile hold the long chain

1x1 round plate looks like a lava bubble

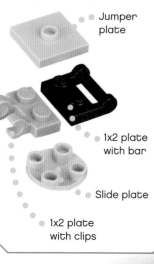

Steps help to support the bridge

Flame elements attach to transparent cones

VILLAGE SHOP

This abandoned shop is filled with crates of untouched goods. It makes the most of ready-made elements, like the crate and ladder. The rear wall is even made from one printed panel with log bricks on either side.

Golden blades on roof

Long LEGO® Technic brick holds rear wall together

REAR VIEW

The roof is fitted with two hinge plates so that it can open up.

Ladder clips onto plate with handled bar

Printed panel shows ancient Ninja masters

2x4 tile attached with clips to a bar

Round brick and tile makes a jar

龍
神

Vegetables in ready-made crate

WARNING SiGNS

It looks like the Ninja are on the right track as they leave the village: there are terrifying Anacondrai warning signs lining the pathway! Signs don't frighten the Ninja of Fire though. Kai has a red-hot glider to help him speed his way to the top of the volcano. The other Ninja grab some weapons and follow Kai on foot.

THINGS ARE HOTTING UP AROUND HERE!

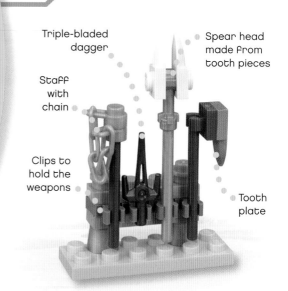

Triple-bladed dagger

Spear head made from tooth pieces

Staff with chain

Clips to hold the weapons

Tooth plate

WEAPONS RACK

This simple rack has cone pieces for legs, and four plates with clips sandwiched between two plates. There is room for a staff fitted with a chain, a spear with two giant teeth, and an ax with a downward-facing claw.

This sign is built up using layers of black plates, including plates with vertical clips, which can hold bones or even snakes. Don't build your sign too big, or it might tip over!

Plates with clips attach banners to these swords

龍神

龍神

Brick with side studs fits onto staff

SIGNPOSTS

A collection of intimidating warning signs greets the Ninja on their trail! They all start with textured round bricks on a broad base, but they all look very different. Poles, spears, printed tiles, horns, skulls, bones, and even snakes can all help to create a scary sign.

Pole slots into round brick

Large base makes a stable structure

Base covered with 1x1 slopes to look like glowing lava

Wing glides above the fiery lava

1x2 plate with long bar attaches to the bottom of a 2x2 curved plate

A hinge cylinder connects the glider and tail

FIRE GLIDER

Kai's blazing fire glider has dragon claws for wings and extra-long tail fins made from bars with plates. Both the wings and tail fins are attached with click-hinge cylinders, allowing them to move up and down.

DRAGON CLAW WINGS

Two LEGO Technic levers clip into each claw wing piece, with a red LEGO Technic pin through the top holes. The other half of the pin fits into a hinge cylinder, in turn attached to a hinge plate built into the model.

Hinge plate

Click hinge plate

Hinge cylinder

Wu's hat piece fits on to angled plate using a 1x1 round plate underneath

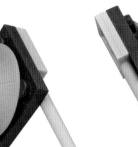

Steering wheel piece comes with its own base

Symbol of the phoenix—a creature born out of the ashes of a fire

If you don't have these clawed wings, try making up your own

SERPENT STRIKE

Few people have ever been this far up the volcano, so the Ninja are surprised to see a grand gateway amid the glowing, molten rocks. Is it the way in to another Anacondrai hideout? There's only one way to find out. The Ninja go through, only to find that an enormous serpent guards this particular route!

WOAH! HE'S A BIG FELLA!

WHAT WILL YOU BUILD?

- Drawbridge and gates
- Winding rocky path
- Red-hot stones
- Sentry guard
- Phoenix

LAVA GATEWAY

It's easy to make a decorative entrance with very simple shapes. This gateway uses angled plates attached to a central round plate. Its pillars are built onto small sentry boxes, with a window frame piece for the sentry to see out of—but it looks like no one is home!

Transparent 1x1 slopes are glistening hot lava

Gray sloped bricks of different sizes look like rocks

Angled plate fitted sideways at the top of the entrance

Flames pieces attach to plates with clips

Hinge plate puts the lava walls at an angle

Window frame element

Long, pointed
horn piece

HINGED BODY

A mix of joints can make a model move in a variety
of ways. A ball-and-socket joint allows this serpent's
head to move in any direction, and another joins
the raised neck to the long body. These joints are
designed to be quite stiff, so you can pose your
model and keep it balanced. The tail sections are
linked with click hinges, which also add movement,
but don't move in all directions like ball joints do.

Ball-and-
socket
joint

1x1 slopes
make spiky
sides

Click hinge allows
tail to lash out
at the Ninja

Jaw opens to
reveal the
beast's fangs

Hinge cylinder
connects tail

Curved pieces
cover the
creature's back

Flames leap
from the fire
serpent's body

FIRE SERPENT

Rising from the burning lava comes a flaming
fire serpent. Its head is a triangular shape made
using angled pieces and curved slopes. The
winding tail segments need a broad base to
keep the creature's large head stable.

Set the
tooth
plate at
an angle

Create the fire serpent's
fearsome eye using a black plate
fitted with a bright yellow tooth
plate. Add car mudguards above
and below to encase the eye.

Curved half
arches make
a rounded
shape for
the neck

SIDE VIEW OF HEAD

READY FOR BATTLE

Beyond the fire serpent, the Ninja find out what it was defending: an Anacondrai base where the snakes and their soldiers are making new and unusual weapons. The base is protected by a missile launcher, ready to spew venom at the Ninja. Lucky that Kai has a blazing set of wheels to take it on!

WHAT D'YOU MEAN I'M HOT HEADED?

FLICK-FIRE VENOM

An Anacondrai soldier stands on a 4x4 round plate fastened to a radar dish at the top of this missile station. From his high vantage point, he controls flick-fire missiles held in LEGO Technic beams.

Printed curved element

Transparent bars make drips of toxic venom

LEGO Technic beam with stick holds flick-fire missiles

WEAPONS FORGE

There are two parts to the snakes' weapon-making forge. On one side is a roaring fire for heating up metal. On the other is an anvil for shaping the weapons. Try expanding a scene like this by building a workbench or stable.

Butterfly sword piece

The fire pit is contained by brick walls. The walls hide the 1x1 plates with vertical clips that hold the flames.

Telescope extends the triple-bladed dagger

Slope brick for chimney

Anvil built around 1x1 brick with side studs

Four flame pieces make a roaring fire

An A-plate connects the two parts

Before fitting the windshield, make sure the cockpit is deep enough and wide enough to hold a minifigure.

FIRE CAR

Kai's super-tough fire car has a chunky wheel at the back and two smaller wheels at the front. The rear wheel is attached to the body of the car with a LEGO Technic axle threaded through two long LEGO Technic bricks with holes.

Shuriken attaches to faucet element

Three robot arms link the cockpit lid and windshield

Wheels attach to this long LEGO Technic brick with holes

Blades are positioned to avoid touching the wheels

GRILLE ATTACHMENT

This barred fence makes a great big radiator grille. Two plates with clips fix it to the car, while other clips are used to attach cool accessories including a control panel tile. Three robot arms connect the windshield to the grille.

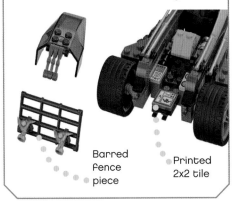

Barred fence piece

Printed 2x2 tile

Blades protect sides of vehicle

Flames attached to LEGO Technic pin fix to 1x1 brick with hole

REAR VIEW

Hinge cylinder holds flame

TEMPLE SHOWDOWN

At the top of the volcano, the Ninja discover an ancient temple that towers above the bubbling lava. The Anacondrai have made this their new base for building their mech—and they are very nearly finished!

DON'T LOOK UP, NINJA! HEE HEE HEE!

They battle the Ninja and escape once more. Things are really hotting up now...

WHAT WILL YOU BUILD?

- Lava-proof sailing boat
- Fire temple statues
- Hot-air balloon
- Wall of flame
- Lava flow

2x4 ridged roof slopes

Flame slots into end of tail piece

Golden dragon talon connects to a lance piece

Tail piece slots into LEGO Technic brick with hole

FIRE TEMPLE

This impressive temple is ablaze with torches and bristling with blades. It rises up from a base of lava-colored plates on pillars supported by rocky slope bricks. Its top room seems to be a peaceful shrine, but a fiery surprise is hidden in the roof space above!

10x4 plate leads up to temple

Hinge cylinder holds the talons at an angle

ACTION VIEW

Roof opens on hinge bricks

Roof space filled with lava bombs

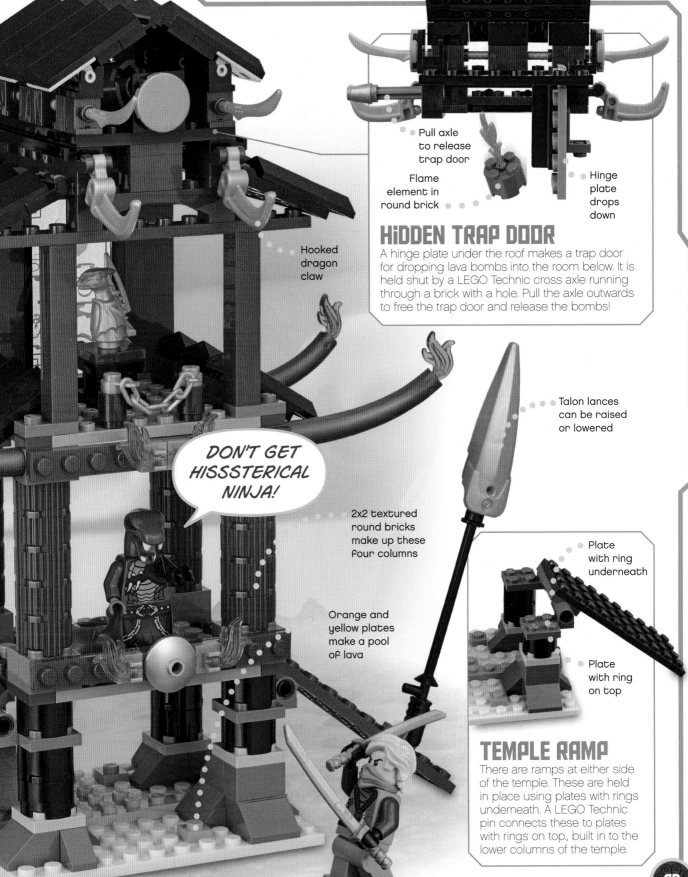

Pull axle
to release
trap door

Flame
element in
round brick

Hinge
plate
drops
down

HiDDEN TRAP DOOR

A hinge plate under the roof makes a trap door
for dropping lava bombs into the room below. It is
held shut by a LEGO Technic cross axle running
through a brick with a hole. Pull the axle outwards
to free the trap door and release the bombs!

Hooked
dragon
claw

Talon lances
can be raised
or lowered

DON'T GET
HISSSTERICAL
NINJA!

2x2 textured
round bricks
make up these
four columns

Plate
with ring
underneath

Orange and
yellow plates
make a pool
of lava

Plate
with ring
on top

TEMPLE RAMP

There are ramps at either side
of the temple. These are held
in place using plates with rings
underneath. A LEGO Technic
pin connects these to plates
with rings on top., built in to the
lower columns of the temple.

THE BiG FREEZE

The Ninja have come a long way since the Anacondrai stole their mech blueprints. Now they have traced their enemies to the freezing mountains. Everything here is covered in a thick layer of snow and ice—

IT'S COLDER THAN SENSEI'S ICED TEA!

and is very, very slippery! Surely this must be the setting for their final showdown?

SNOWY LANDSCAPE

Only the toughest plants can survive in the mountains. Use white round bricks and radar dishes to make snow-covered trees and bamboo plants.

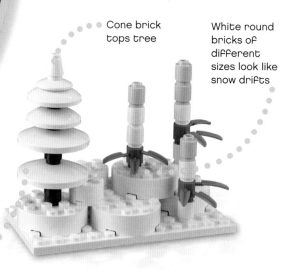

Cone brick tops tree

White round bricks of different sizes look like snow drifts

Round bricks and radar dishes make a snowy tree

FROZEN IN

Stay in the mountains too long and you might get frozen in—like this unfortunate skeleton! Though perhaps he isn't quite as trapped as he appears... Pull the lever on the side and he can break free!

I'M CHILLED TO THE BONE!

Two clear rock pieces form the block of ice

There is room for a skeleton (or a Ninja!) inside

ICE ESCAPE

A lever under your block of ice means you can break it open and free whoever is trapped inside. This one uses a LEGO® Technic angled connector as a lever. A LEGO Technic pin holds it in place. A smooth tile under the ice helps it break away easily.

Flip this LEGO Technic lever to break the ice

ACTION VIEW

Two studs hold the front of the ice in place

FOUNTAIN CLIMB

Water is precious in this frozen landscape. This fountain must be built on a hot spring! Zane must climb a steep ramp to reach it. The ramp is held in place using LEGO Technic pins. Large rock pieces make stable sides for the whole structure.

Transparent blue bars make great icicles

Blue flame element set in an upturned radar dish makes a water fountain

Round tile with hole

SLIPPERY SLOPE

The steep slope up to the fountain is a 10x6 plate. Underneath it are a pair of 2x2 plates with rings underneath. LEGO Technic pins connect these to plates with rings on top. This allows the ramp to be set at an angle.

LEGO Technic pin slots into plate with ring on top

Large plant leaf piece

Inverted slope supports arch above

IT'S MORE SLIPPERY THAN AN ANACONDRAI!

A horn slots into a brick with side studs to make this tree trunk

White tiles are slippery like ice

Plates with vertical bars make hand-holds for the Ninja

SNAKE SURPRISE

It's not easy struggling through the snow and ice, but it all seems worthwhile when Jay finds a treasure chest! There's something very odd about it being here, though, and Zane is the first to suspect a trap. He leaps into action just in time as the Anacondrai launch their latest attack on the Ninja!

THIS IS TREASURE BEYOND MEASURE!

TREASURE CHEST

This box of treasure is marked with a flag attached to a pole. A variety of curved and slope bricks forms the snowy base and the box has hinges for each side of its lid. Fill it with small colored bricks and other treasure!

Flagpole slots into 1x1 cone brick

Edge plates at both ends of the box stop the treasure from falling out

The base of the box is a 4x4 plate and the lid is two 2x4 tiles. Hinge bricks under each tile allow it to open and close.

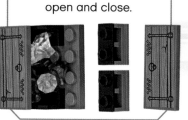

A pair of 1x1 slopes hold the treasure box in place

SNAKE SNOWMOBILE

No sooner have the Ninja seen the treasure than the Anacondrai attack! Their super-speedy snowmobile has blade-like skis to scythe through the snow—and flick-fire missiles to target any unwary Ninja!

Long tail fixes to a 2x2 plate with a hole

A 1x2 hinge brick adds a tilt to the curved brick at the front of the vehicle. Underneath, 1x2 plates hold the skis in place.

Flick-fire missiles made from long LEGO Technic pins

Missiles slot into a LEGO Technic beam with stick

ICE GLIDER

The Anacondrai should know better than to challenge Zane while on the ice! His powerful ice glider can speed across the frozen landscape and has cannons, swords, and pincers to defend against snake attack from all sides!

WHAT WILL YOU BUILD?

- Anacondrai snowman
- 4x4 snowmobile
- Ice sculptures
- Snow plow
- Ski slope

REAR DEFENSES

Two rows of golden blades protect the back of the ice glider. They slot into six gold robot arms that clip on to two plates with angled bars. The plates with angled bars are fixed sideways to plates with brackets—as are the three domes at the back.

REAR VIEW

Icy blue 1x1 slopes add a dash of color

Clip plates on either side can hold a pair of sai weapons

Blades can move from side to side

Plate with angled bars

Hidden cannons extend from 2x2 round bricks held together with LEGO Technic axles

Shooter arm serves as a defensive pincer

2x16 rotor blades conceal the mighty cannons

73

ICE FORTRESS

As the Ninja make their way up the mountain, they know they're getting close to the Anacondrai's icy base. First they find an igloo where someone has been recently, and then Cole sees a terrifying frozen fortress with huge snake skulls on either side of the door! Do they dare go in?

ANYONE WOULD THINK WE WEREN'T WELCOME!

IGLOO

The cold Ninja are glad to find a warming fire inside this igloo, but it means someone must have been here recently! Four quarter domes make up the roof, held together with round plates.

1x1 slopes hold roof in place

Two arched bricks form an entrance

Mostly white bricks suggest snow and ice

Use hinge plates for lower jaw so mouth can open and close

A mix of tiles and plates hold the roof in place but make it easy to lift off, revealing the fire.

Will Cole get past the guard?

Sloped bricks and plates with teeth look like snow and ice

GUARD POST

This defensive barrier is made from two rows of long plates connected in the middle with hinge plates. It is attached to the 2x12 plate beneath with headlight bricks turned at an angle so that the barrier points outwards.

WHAT WILL YOU BUILD?

- Snowball launcher
- Frozen fishpond
- Yeti in its lair
- Ice tower
- Ski lift

FORTRESS

Only the Anacondrai would build such a scary base! With its watchful guard and moving snake skulls on both sides of the door, it looks like they don't want any visitors...

Rows of 1x2 log bricks make up the roof

Eyes are 2x2 round plates, just visible through this gap

Build the skull around a ball joint so it can move in any direction. Use angle plates to build the jaw and cheekbones sideways.

Sides can close like a snake's jaw thanks to this hinge plate

Bricks with side studs hold each side of the entrance in place

Row of blades attached to four 1x1 bricks with side studs

INTO THE ARENA

The entrance to the fortress is too heavily guarded to simply walk right in. So Zane uses his ice hovercraft to look from above and spots a second, secret door. The five Ninja sneak in, only to find the Anacondrai waiting for them, in an arena set up for a special battle. "Welcome to the war of the mechsss," they hiss!

SSSO, YOU'RE HERE AT LASSST, NINJA!

BATTLE ARENA

What sort of combat was this battle arena built for? It's a large outdoor space at the heart of the Anacondrai fortress, capped with snow and ice. With weapons racks on either side, it seems to be set up for a battle between two mechs!

Use a 3x3x6 cylinder brick to make these columns. Complete the shape with slopes and a jumper plate, then top with a white radar dish to suggest snow. Decorate with 1x1 round tiles and fiery horns on a clip plate.

Cylinder brick

Bones add to scary battle atmosphere

Robot claw in round brick holds sword

All kinds of white elements can be used to create a wintry scene. Try using arches, curved and slope bricks, radar dishes, angled plates, and even horns and plates with teeth.

Club made from horns fixed to brick with side studs and stand

This A-plate holds both sides of the arena at an angle

LET'SSS RUMBLE!

PROPELLERS

Zane's ice chopper has two sets of spinnng rotor blades. Each propeller is attached to a 2x2 pin-top plate, and surrounded by a protective housing made from dragon claws and transparent blue curved windscreens.

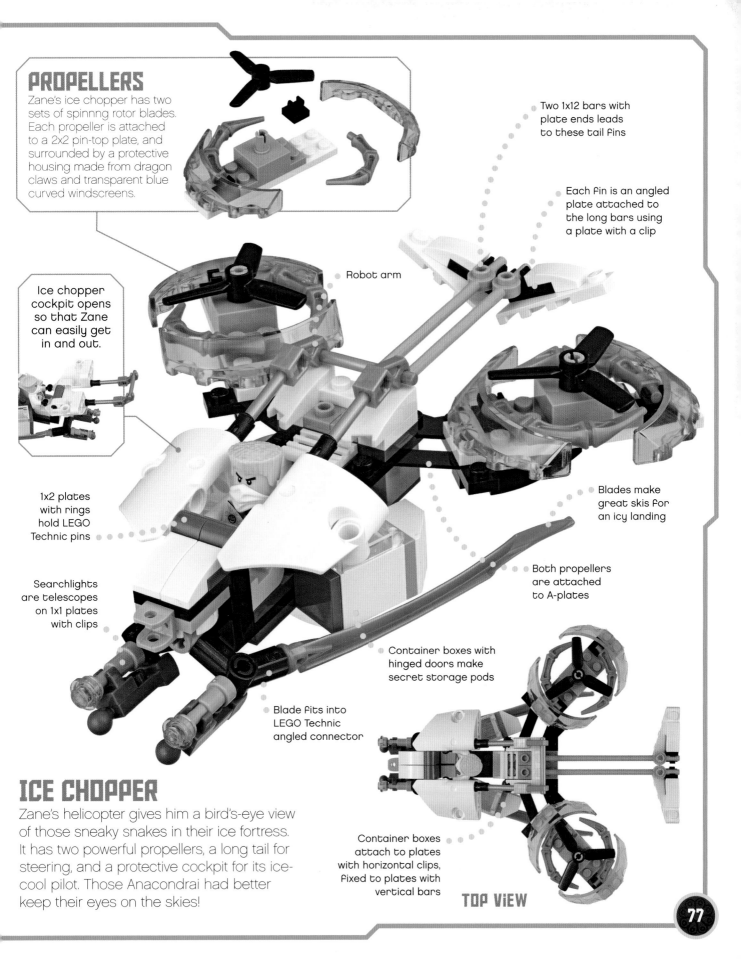

Two 1x12 bars with plate ends leads to these tail fins

Each fin is an angled plate attached to the long bars using a plate with a clip

Robot arm

Ice chopper cockpit opens so that Zane can easily get in and out.

1x2 plates with rings hold LEGO Technic pins

Blades make great skis for an icy landing

Searchlights are telescopes on 1x1 plates with clips

Both propellers are attached to A-plates

Container boxes with hinged doors make secret storage pods

Blade fits into LEGO Technic angled connector

ICE CHOPPER

Zane's helicopter gives him a bird's-eye view of those sneaky snakes in their ice fortress. It has two powerful propellers, a long tail for steering, and a protective cockpit for its ice-cool pilot. Those Anacondrai had better keep their eyes on the skies!

Container boxes attach to plates with horizontal clips, fixed to plates with vertical bars

TOP VIEW

MECH SHOWDOWN

The Anacondrai have completed their mech! Now the Ninja can see what they're up against. Their enemies haven't just copied the stolen mech plans—they've added a whole new snake-like spin on them! Lloyd is ready in his Green Ninja mech. The battle is on, and there can be only one winner!

MY MECH IS BETTER THAN YOUR MECH!

THIS IS A LEAN, GREEN MACHINE!

Two seats make this protective breastplate

Huge Ninja blades

Armor made from window shutter

Ball joints on both hips

Smaller ball joints at ankles

Mech towers over charging platform

1x6x5 girder

2x2 tile on brick with side studs

GREEN NINJA MECH

Lloyd is well protected in his Ninja mech. Shields fold down on hinge bricks, and mighty jointed arms wield blades that only a mech could lift! Its legs also have armor plating and are capable of huge strides.

MECH PLATFORM

The mech powers up for battle at this high-tech docking station. Girder pieces form the back wall and two lattice plates make up the floor. It has control panels on both sides and a chunky pipe for pumping the mech energy!

Plates with clips and plates with bars make hinged joints

Ball-and-socket joint

Round tile with hole

Angle plate

BLASTER GUNS

Four 1x1 round bricks make the barrels of each blaster. Top them with a 2x2 round plate, then add a 2x2 round tile with a hole. This attaches upside-down to a jumper plate, which fits onto an angle plate. Attach this to a ball-and-socket joint, so the weapon can move around.

BOO! HISS! ESPECIALLY HISS!

Click hinges connect both ends of this body segment

Tail piece fits into this LEGO Technic brick with a hole

1x1 slopes and 1x2 tiles make smooth scales

Two ball-and-socket joints enable this segment to move

SNAKE MECH

No one has ever seen a mech like this before! It has the body and head of a serpent, plus all the firepower of a small army. An Anacondrai henchman fits inside—underneath a pair of terrifying fangs!

Curved body is built sideways using hidden angle plates

I'M OUT OF HERE!

Sloped brick hides two plates with click hinges

NINJA VICTORY

It's a tough battle when mech meets mech, but it's soon clear that Lloyd has the upper hand! His Green Ninja mech easily stands up to the snake mech's blaster bolts—and his swords are a match for the sharpest fangs. As the defeated Anacondrai slink away, the Ninja agree never to leave their plans lying around again!

Penguin
Random
House

Senior Editor Hannah Dolan
Additional Editor Scarlett O'Hara
Editorial Assistant Beth Davies
Senior Art Editors Samantha Richiardi
and Lisa Sodeau
Project Art Editor Lauren Adams
Senior Pre-Production Producer Marc Staples
Senior Producer Lloyd Robertson
Managing Editor Simon Hugo
Design Manager Guy Harvey
Art Director Lisa Lanzarini
Publisher Julie Ferris
Publishing Director Simon Beecroft

Written by Scarlett O'Hara
Inspirational models built by Barney Main
Photography by Gary Ombler

Dorling Kindersley would like to thank Randi Sørensen,
Simon Lucas, Adrian Florea, Henk van der Does, Paul Hansford,
Robert Ekblom, and Alexandra Martin at the LEGO Group.
Thanks also to Matt Jones for editorial assistance and
Rhys Thomas and Sam Bartlett for design assistance at DK.

First published in the United States in 2015
by DK Publishing, 345 Hudson Street,
New York, New York 10014
A Penguin Random House Company

19 10 9 8 7 6 5
024–185655–Aug/15

DK books are available at special discounts when purchased
in bulk for sales promotions, premiums, fund-raising, or
educational use. For details, contact: DK Publishing Special
Markets, 345 Hudson Street, New York, New York 10014
SpecialSales@dk.com

A CIP catalog record for this book is available
from the Library of Congress.

ISBN: 978-1-4654-3590-3

Color reproduction by
Tranistics Data Technologies Pvt. Ltd.
Printed and bound in China

www.LEGO.com
www.dk.com

A WORLD OF IDEAS:
SEE ALL THERE IS TO KNOW

龍神 龍神